AMAZING
SPACE Q&A

Author Dr. Mike Goldsmith
Consultant Jacqueline Mitton

DK

**LONDON, NEW YORK,
MELBOURNE, MUNICH, and DELHI**

Senior Art Editors Smiljka Surla, Jane Thomas
Designer Daniela Boraschi
Additional Designers Hoa Luc, Johnny Pau
Senior Editor Shaila Brown
Managing Editor Linda Esposito
Managing Art Editor Jim Green

Category Publisher Laura Buller
Design Development Manager Sophia M. Tampakopoulos
Production Controller Charlotte Oliver
Production Editor Marc Staples
DK Picture Library Claire Bowers
Picture Researcher Karen VanRoss
Additional Picture Researcher Myriam Megharbi

Jacket Editor Matilda Gollon
Jacket Designer Laura Brim

Published in the United States in 2011
by DK Publishing, 375 Hudson Street, New York, New York 10014

DK books are available at special discounts when purchased in bulk for sales
promotions, premiums, fund-raising, or educational use. For details, contact:
DK Publishing Special Markets, 375 Hudson Street, New York, New York 10014,
or SpecialSales@dk.com.

A catalog record for this book is available
from the Library of Congress.

ISBN 978-0-7566-7130-3

Hi-res workflow proofed by MDP, UK
Printed and bound in China by Toppan

**Discover more at
www.dk.com**

CONTENTS

IN THE BEGINNING

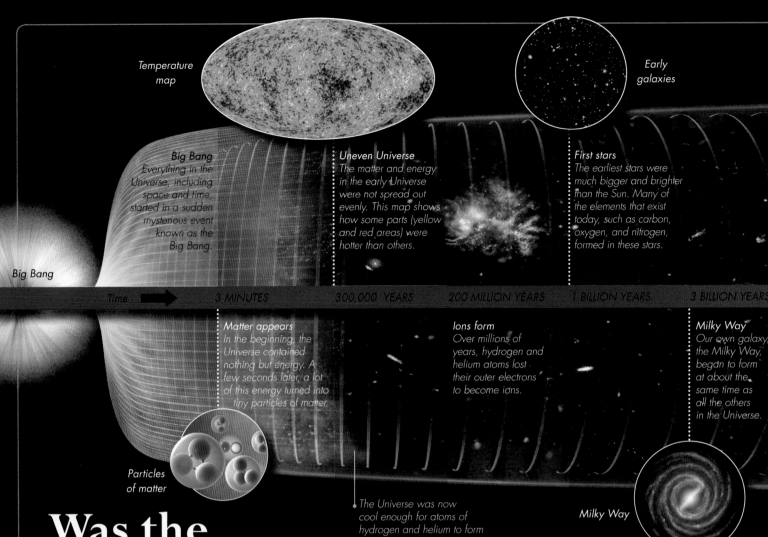

Temperature map

Early galaxies

Big Bang

Big Bang
Everything in the Universe, including space and time, started in a sudden mysterious event known as the Big Bang.

Uneven Universe
The matter and energy in the early Universe were not spread out evenly. This map shows how some parts (yellow and red areas) were hotter than others.

First stars
The earliest stars were much bigger and brighter than the Sun. Many of the elements that exist today, such as carbon, oxygen, and nitrogen, formed in these stars.

Time → | 3 MINUTES | 300,000 YEARS | 200 MILLION YEARS | 1 BILLION YEARS | 3 BILLION YEARS

Matter appears
In the beginning, the Universe contained nothing but energy. A few seconds later, a lot of this energy turned into tiny particles of matter.

Ions form
Over millions of years, hydrogen and helium atoms lost their outer electrons to become ions.

Milky Way
Our own galaxy, the Milky Way, began to form at about the same time as all the others in the Universe.

Particles of matter

The Universe was now cool enough for atoms of hydrogen and helium to form

Milky Way

Was the Big Bang loud?

The Big Bang was not a sound. It was the beginning of the Universe, in which enormous amounts of energy appeared and space itself expanded suddenly. Since then, the Universe has continued to expand and cool. Scientists do not yet understand what caused the Big Bang, but they have theories about how today's Universe developed from it.

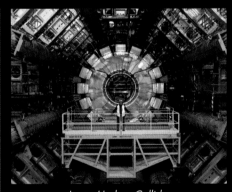
Large Hadron Collider

Q A **What is the Universe?**
The Universe is everything that exists. Everything in it is either matter or energy. The objects you see around you are made of matter. Air and water are types of matter, too. Energy exists in many forms, including sound, light, heat, and motion. A lot of the matter in the Universe is gathered together to form stars, which exist in groups called galaxies. These galaxies also form groups.

Group of galaxies

Q A **How do scientists study the Universe?**
Scientists use telescopes, computers, and other specialized equipment to study the Universe. At a laboratory called CERN in Switzerland, scientists use the Large Hadron Collider to accelerate particles to enormous speeds in order to study the way tiny particles of matter were formed and destroyed in the early Universe.

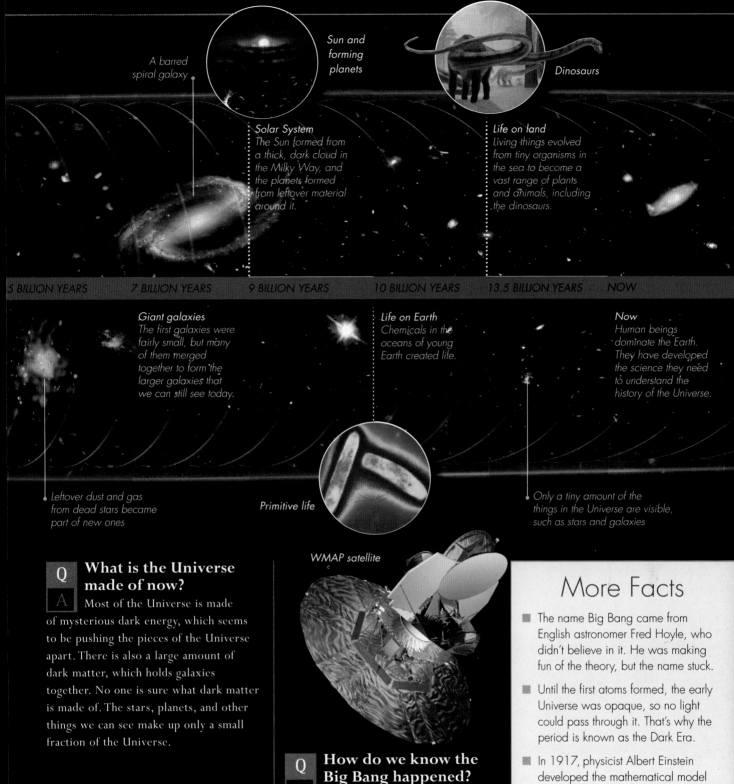

A barred spiral galaxy

Sun and forming planets

Dinosaurs

Solar System
The Sun formed from a thick, dark cloud in the Milky Way, and the planets formed from leftover material around it.

Life on land
Living things evolved from tiny organisms in the sea to become a vast range of plants and animals, including the dinosaurs.

5 BILLION YEARS   7 BILLION YEARS   9 BILLION YEARS   10 BILLION YEARS   13.5 BILLION YEARS   NOW

Giant galaxies
The first galaxies were fairly small, but many of them merged together to form the larger galaxies that we can still see today.

Life on Earth
Chemicals in the oceans of young Earth created life.

Now
Human beings dominate the Earth. They have developed the science they need to understand the history of the Universe.

Leftover dust and gas from dead stars became part of new ones

Primitive life

Only a tiny amount of the things in the Universe are visible, such as stars and galaxies

WMAP satellite

Q A What is the Universe made of now?

Most of the Universe is made of mysterious dark energy, which seems to be pushing the pieces of the Universe apart. There is also a large amount of dark matter, which holds galaxies together. No one is sure what dark matter is made of. The stars, planets, and other things we can see make up only a small fraction of the Universe.

Atoms 5%   Dark matter 23%

Contents of the Universe

Dark energy 72%

Q A How do we know the Big Bang happened?

The Big Bang involved a huge burst of energy. We know the Big Bang happened because some of this energy still exists, filling the whole Universe with energy. This energy is called cosmic microwave background radiation, and it can be measured and mapped by satellites, such as the Wilkinson Microwave Anisotropy Probe (WMAP), which orbit high above Earth, where there is no atmosphere to obstruct their observations.

More Facts

- The name Big Bang came from English astronomer Fred Hoyle, who didn't believe in it. He was making fun of the theory, but the name stuck.

- Until the first atoms formed, the early Universe was opaque, so no light could pass through it. That's why the period is known as the Dark Era.

- In 1917, physicist Albert Einstein developed the mathematical model of the Universe that is still used today. Belgian astronomer Georges Lemaître suggested the Big Bang theory ten years later.

Georges Lemaître (left) and Albert Einstein

How do we know the Universe is expanding?

When a glowing object moves away from us, its light is slightly redder than usual. Measurements of clusters of galaxies show that their light is reddened, so we know that they are moving away from us. The whole Universe is expanding, with all its clusters of galaxies getting farther and farther apart.

Q A Do scientists fully understand the Universe?
Many theories of the Universe are still being developed. For instance, although we know that the structures we see today, such as galaxies and superclusters, started as areas of different temperature in the early Universe, it is hard to explain what actually caused these differences, and the cause of the Big Bang itself is still a mystery.

Coolest regions are blue

Temperature map of the early Universe

The most distant galaxies are the reddest

Q A Who discovered that the Universe is expanding?
In the 1910s, American astronomer Vesto Slipher discovered that the light from some galaxies was reddened. By the 1920s, American astronomer Edwin Hubble had found a way to work out the distances of galaxies, so he and fellow astronomer Milton Humason compared the amounts of reddening with these distances. They discovered that more distant galaxies were moving away faster. This suggested that the Universe was expanding.

Q A How fast is the Universe expanding?
The speed at which a cluster of galaxies is moving depends on how far away it is—the farther away, the faster it goes. The table below shows three galaxy clusters: Hydra, Corona Borealis, and Virgo. Hydra is nearly three times as far as Corona Borealis, and it is moving nearly three times as fast. Compared to these two galaxy clusters, Virgo is nearby and moving relatively slowly.

Edwin Hubble

More Facts

- The study of the whole Universe, which is also known as the cosmos, is called cosmology.

- It is possible that there are other Universes separate from our own.

- Theories of the Universe assume that, at a very early stage in its history, there was a sudden, enormous burst of expansion called inflation. However, no one can explain why it happened.

- Before science, early civilizations had many myths about the Universe. Ancient Egyptians, for example, believed that the body of the goddess Nut formed the starry sky.

Egyptian painting of the goddess Nut

Virgo	Corona Borealis	Hydra
Cluster	**Distance in light years (ly)**	**Speed (per second)**
Virgo	55 million ly	740 miles (1,200 km)
Corona Borealis	1 billion ly	13,600 miles (22,000 km)
Hydra	2.8 billion ly	37,900 miles (61,000 km)

Diagram shows the possible fates of the Universe

Time

Big Chill: The Universe expands slowly and forever, cooling until everything dies

Modified Big Chill: Expansion speeds up as time passes

Big Crunch: The Universe collapses and ends in a burst of energy

Big Rip: Everything in the Universe eventually tears itself apart

The Universe at present

Big Bang

Q How will the Universe end?

A Most scientists think the Universe will end in one of two ways—either the galaxies, stars, and atoms that make up the Universe will rip themselves apart eventually, or the Universe will expand forever, gradually cooling until it is completely dark and dead. It is also possible that the Universe will stop expanding over time and crash back in on itself. These three theories are known as the Big Rip, Big Chill, and Big Crunch.

A quasar

Q Does the Universe have an edge?

A Early astronomers thought that somewhere beyond the stars there was an end to the Universe, but now we know that no matter how far and fast you traveled through the Universe, you would never reach an edge. Some theories of the Universe suggest that it has only a limited volume, which means that you might eventually return to your starting point if you traveled for long enough.

A woodcut imagining an edge to the Universe

Q How big is the Universe?

A Light travels at the incredible speed of 180,000 miles (300,000 km) per second. A light year is the distance that light travels in a year—about 6 trillion miles (10 trillion km). The Universe is at least 90 billion light years across. The most distant objects we can see are either remote galaxies or quasars. A quasar is an enormously bright light, thought to be caused by matter falling into a black hole in the heart of a distant galaxy.

Q What is the Solar System?

A The Solar System consists of the Sun, Earth, and seven other planets, and many smaller worlds, together with rocks, dust, and gases. All the worlds in the Solar System spin, and all of them are in orbit either around the Sun itself or around other worlds. Nearly all the mass of the Solar System is contained in the Sun.

The Solar System is shown here at three different scales

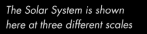

Oort Cloud

Kuiper Belt

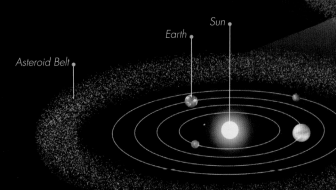

Sun

Earth

Asteroid Belt

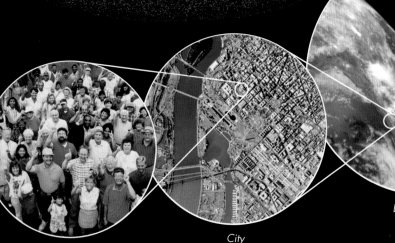

Inner Solar System

Earth and Moon

City

Us

Where do we fit in?

We live on a small planet called Earth, about 8,000 miles (13,000 km) across. Earth is one of four rocky planets, also called the inner planets because they are in the inner part of the Solar System. Beyond the inner planets is a belt of asteroids and four giant planets. At the center of the Solar System is the Sun. The Sun is a member of a large spiral galaxy, the Milky Way, which is one of a group of galaxies called the Local Group. The Local Group, along with other groups and clusters of galaxies, forms a supercluster.

Q Where are we in the Solar System?

A Our planet Earth is the third planet from the Sun, and only about 93 million miles (150 million km) away from it. This means that we are much closer to the Sun than most of the Solar System, the outer regions of which are trillions of miles away. Our closeness to the Sun means Earth is warmer and brighter than most of the worlds of the Solar System.

From space, the Sun has a pinkish tint

Sun shining on Earth

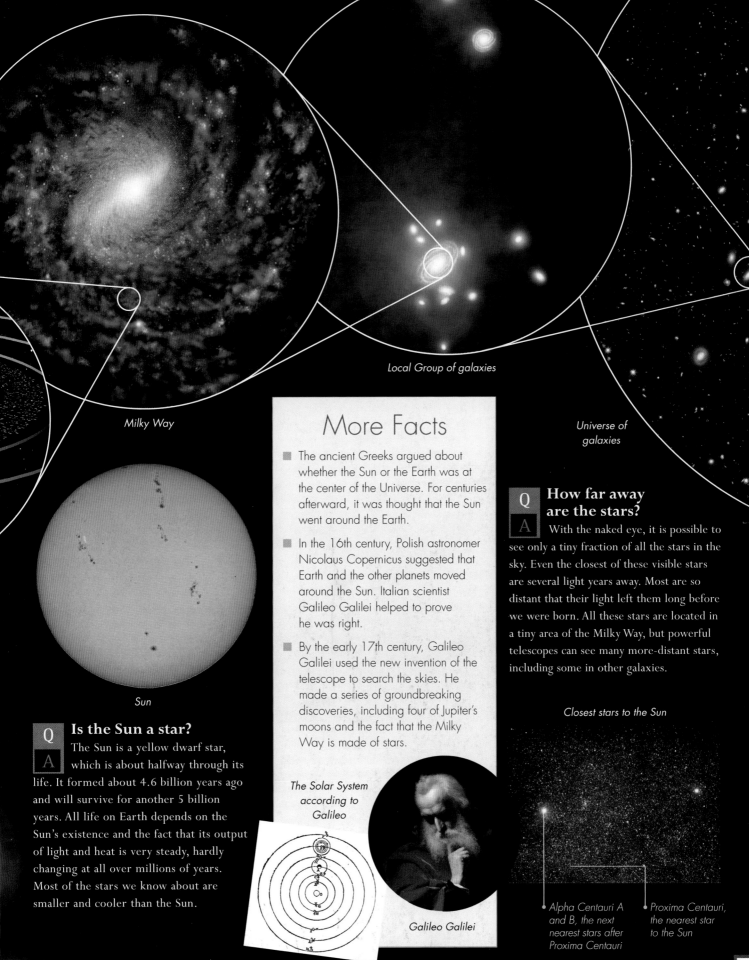

Milky Way

Local Group of galaxies

Universe of galaxies

Sun

More Facts

■ The ancient Greeks argued about whether the Sun or the Earth was at the center of the Universe. For centuries afterward, it was thought that the Sun went around the Earth.

■ In the 16th century, Polish astronomer Nicolaus Copernicus suggested that Earth and the other planets moved around the Sun. Italian scientist Galileo Galilei helped to prove he was right.

■ By the early 17th century, Galileo Galilei used the new invention of the telescope to search the skies. He made a series of groundbreaking discoveries, including four of Jupiter's moons and the fact that the Milky Way is made of stars.

The Solar System according to Galileo

Galileo Galilei

Q A Is the Sun a star?

The Sun is a yellow dwarf star, which is about halfway through its life. It formed about 4.6 billion years ago and will survive for another 5 billion years. All life on Earth depends on the Sun's existence and the fact that its output of light and heat is very steady, hardly changing at all over millions of years. Most of the stars we know about are smaller and cooler than the Sun.

Q A How far away are the stars?

With the naked eye, it is possible to see only a tiny fraction of all the stars in the sky. Even the closest of these visible stars are several light years away. Most are so distant that their light left them long before we were born. All these stars are located in a tiny area of the Milky Way, but powerful telescopes can see many more-distant stars, including some in other galaxies.

Closest stars to the Sun

Alpha Centauri A and B, the next nearest stars after Proxima Centauri

Proxima Centauri, the nearest star to the Sun

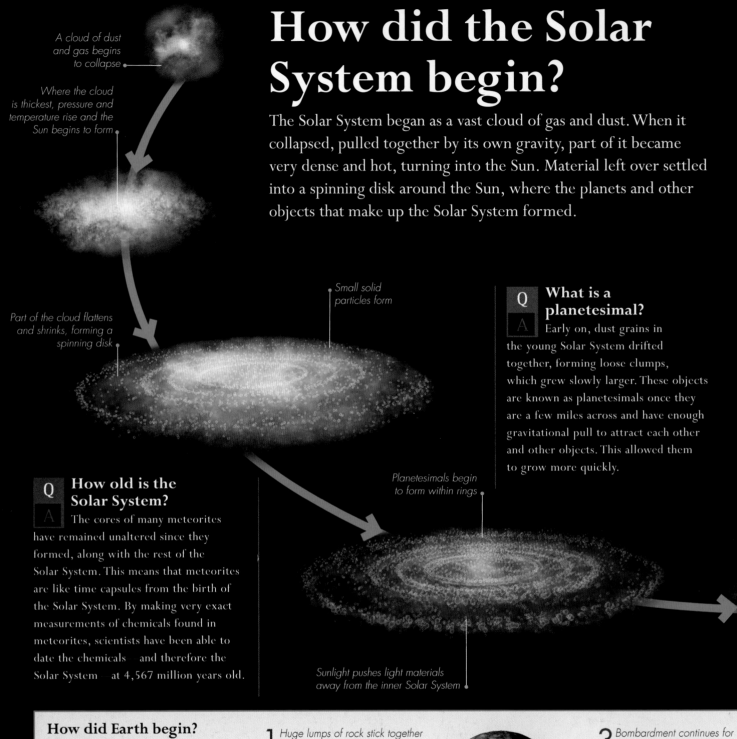

How did the Solar System begin?

The Solar System began as a vast cloud of gas and dust. When it collapsed, pulled together by its own gravity, part of it became very dense and hot, turning into the Sun. Material left over settled into a spinning disk around the Sun, where the planets and other objects that make up the Solar System formed.

A cloud of dust and gas begins to collapse

Where the cloud is thickest, pressure and temperature rise and the Sun begins to form

Part of the cloud flattens and shrinks, forming a spinning disk

Small solid particles form

Planetesimals begin to form within rings

Sunlight pushes light materials away from the inner Solar System

Q **A** **What is a planetesimal?**
Early on, dust grains in the young Solar System drifted together, forming loose clumps, which grew slowly larger. These objects are known as planetesimals once they are a few miles across and have enough gravitational pull to attract each other and other objects. This allowed them to grow more quickly.

Q **A** **How old is the Solar System?**
The cores of many meteorites have remained unaltered since they formed, along with the rest of the Solar System. This means that meteorites are like time capsules from the birth of the Solar System. By making very exact measurements of chemicals found in meteorites, scientists have been able to date the chemicals — and therefore the Solar System — at 4,567 million years old.

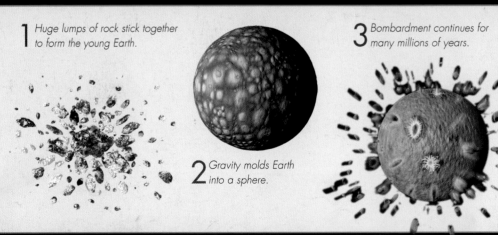

How did Earth begin?

In the early Solar System, many planetesimals crashed into each other, and their gravitational pulls then held them together. As they grew larger, their gravitational pull increased further, drawing more material in and causing them to grow still larger until Earth and its neighboring planets were formed. Long after Earth reached approximately its current size and mass, it continued to be bombarded by material from space.

1 *Huge lumps of rock stick together to form the young Earth.*

2 *Gravity molds Earth into a sphere.*

3 *Bombardment continues for many millions of years.*

Q | Have there always been eight planets?

A | It is thought that dozens of planets around the size of Mercury or Mars once existed. Over a few million years, some of these early planets crashed into each other and stuck together to form some of the planets we see today. It is thought that Earth's Moon was formed after one of these planets collided with Earth.

Q | Did all the planets form at the same time?

A | Astronomers are not sure where or in what order the planets formed, but it is thought that those nearest to the Sun (the rocky planets) formed early in the history of the Solar System, perhaps farther from the Sun than they are now. The giant planets may have formed millions of years later, farther away from the Sun, and then moved out farther still.

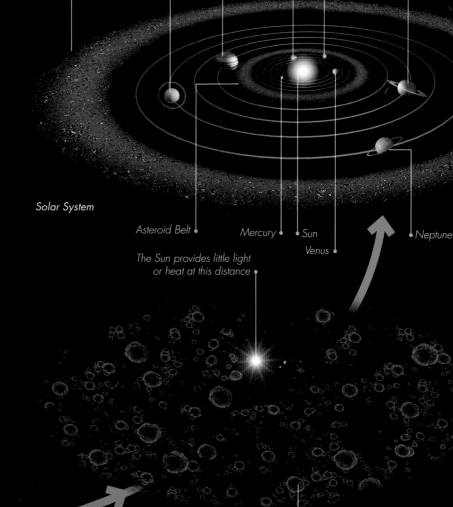

Kuiper Belt

Uranus

Jupiter

Earth

Mars

Saturn

Solar System

Asteroid Belt

Mercury

Sun

Venus

Neptune

The Sun provides little light or heat at this distance

The Sun still partly hidden by dust clouds

Zooming out from the planets, part of the Oort Cloud of icy objects can be seen

Planets begin to form from planetesimals

Q | How big is the Solar System?

A | The Solar System is vast. The Moon is the closest natural object to Earth. Its distance changes as it orbits Earth, from 225,622 miles (363,104 km) at its closest to 252,088 miles (405,696 km) at its farthest point. The farthest planet in the Solar System is 2.8 billion miles (4.5 billion km) from the Sun, and beyond that the Kuiper Belt and Oort Cloud stretch for trillions of miles.

Q | Is the Solar System still changing?

A | Not all of the material that formed the Solar System turned into planets: Some of it remained in the form of asteroids and smaller bodies. Until about 3.8 billion years ago, the planets were frequently struck by these objects, sometimes forming craters. Collisions are now rarer but they still happen—this crater in Arizona was formed only 50,000 years ago.

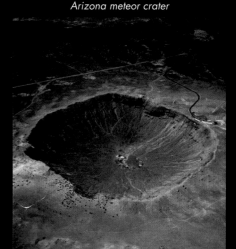

Arizona meteor crater

Earth

Average distance from Earth to Moon: 238,854 miles (384,399 km)

Moon

Neighbors in space

How hot is the Sun?

The Sun is a huge spinning ball of hydrogen and helium, containing 99.9 percent of all the mass in the Solar System. Nuclear fusion reactions in its core produce temperatures of up to 27 million°F (15 million°C). The energy radiates out into the Solar System—bathing the Earth in life-giving light and heat.

Q **What is its surface like?**

A At 9,900°F (5,500°C), the Sun's visible surface, the photosphere, is considerably cooler than the core. It is not solid but made of plasma (ionized gas) that moves in currents and forms "granules" 600 miles (1,000 km) wide. Cooler areas caused by fluctuations in the Sun's magnetic field result in dark sunspots 2,700°F (1,500°C) cooler than the rest of the photosphere. The number of sunspots rises and falls over an 11-year cycle.

Sunspot

Cells of rising gas form granules on the surface

Sunspot

Q **How active is the Sun's atmosphere?**

A Massive eruptions called solar flares send bursts of radiation shooting out into the Solar System, and huge sheets of gas called prominences twist and loop up into the corona over groups of sunspots. Sometimes, huge expanding masses of gas go hurtling out into space; these are called coronal mass ejections. The corona is the outermost layer of atmosphere and is visible from Earth only during a solar eclipse. For reasons no one fully understands, the corona is more than 100 times hotter than the photosphere.

Chromosphere is a layer of hydrogen and helium just above the photosphere

Photosphere is the visible surface

Dense core makes up 2 percent of the Sun's volume but 60 percent of its mass

Solar flare in the Sun's atmosphere

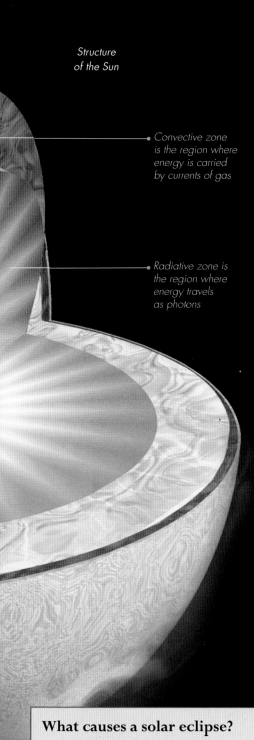

*Structure
of the Sun*

Convective zone
is the region where
energy is carried
by currents of gas

Radiative zone is
the region where
energy travels
as photons

Q A Why does the Sun shine?

The intense heat of the core rips hydrogen atoms apart, leaving only their bare nuclei (centers). The hydrogen nuclei change to helium nuclei in a reaction called nuclear fusion, which releases vast amounts of energy. The energy then travels up through the radiative and convective zones to the surface, where it leaves the Sun as light and heat. Hydrogen-bomb explosions also involve nuclear-fusion reactions.

Aurora Borealis

Q A What is the solar wind?

The solar wind is a stream of tiny particles (electrons and protons) that rushes out of the Sun in all directions. The solar-wind particles can be slowed down by Earth's magnetic field, releasing energy, which we can see as auroras. Auroras are usually seen only from the polar regions. They are called the Aurora Borealis or northern lights in the Northern Hemisphere and the Aurora Australis or southern lights in the Southern Hemisphere.

Hydrogen bomb

Q A Will the Sun last forever?

Our Sun has been shining for 4.6 billion years and will last for at least another 5 billion years, until all the hydrogen fuel in its core is used up. At this point the Sun will cool and become a red giant. After a few million years, the red giant will throw off its outer layers and become a planetary nebula, like the one shown below. Later, when all the gas from the nebula has dispersed, only the Sun's core will remain—a small white dwarf that will slowly cool and darken.

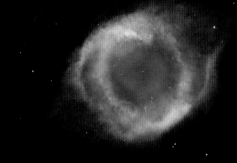

*The Helix Nebula, a planetary nebula
690 light years away from Earth*

What causes a solar eclipse?

When the Sun, Moon, and Earth are directly lined up, the Moon blocks the Sun from view. The Moon casts a shadow on the Earth: people in the dark center (umbra) of the shadow see a total eclipse, while those in the lighter outer shadow (penumbra) see a partial eclipse.

1 *The disk of the Moon appears to creep gradually over the Sun's surface.*

2 *As the eclipse proceeds, more and more of the Sun's surface is covered up.*

3 *When the Sun and Moon are directly aligned, only the Sun's corona is visible.*

4 *As the Sun and Moon move out of alignment, the Sun's disk is revealed again.*

1   2   3   4

More Facts

- On the Moon, things weigh about one-sixth as much as they do on Earth, because the pull of gravity is weaker there.

- The Moon is covered in craters caused by the impact of meteoroids and asteroids. Most of these impacts happened billions of years ago.

- The first science fiction film, made in 1902, was about a trip to the Moon.

Man on the Moon from the 1902 film A Trip to the Moon

Lunar eclipse

The dark areas are huge plains, which were originally thought to be seas but are in fact made of ancient lava

Where did the Moon come from?

This side of the Moon always faces Earth

The Moon was formed about 4.5 billion years ago, following a collision between Earth and an object the size of Mars. A vast amount of rubble was thrown thousands of miles up into space, and some of it went into orbit, forming a great ring around the Earth. Gradually, some of the rubble gathered itself into a sphere, and the sphere grew as it orbited Earth, sweeping up more of the rubble and finally becoming the Moon.

Gravity held the rubble in place as it grew, forming a sphere—the Moon

Formation of the Moon

A huge object struck Earth in a glancing blow

The collision caused great heat, melting some of the material and making it glow brightly in the sky

Some of the rubble formed a doughnut-shaped ring around Earth

As the pieces of rock and dust collided, they stuck together and a single body was formed

What's the difference between a lunar eclipse and a solar eclipse?

In a lunar eclipse, Earth's shadow falls on the Moon, while in a solar eclipse the Moon's shadow falls on Earth. The Moon looks reddish (above right) when it is totally in Earth's shadow because of the way the Sun's light is scattered by Earth's atmosphere.

Astronaut on the Moon

What is gravity?

Gravity is the force that holds you to the ground and prevents Earth from falling apart. It is the force that makes dropped objects fall and keeps the Earth going around the Sun, and the Moon going around the Earth. Gravity operates throughout the whole Universe: The law that describes its strength was discovered in the 17th century by English physicist Isaac Newton, and in the early 20th century it was explained further by German physicist Albert Einstein.

What causes the tides?

The gravitational forces of the Sun and the Moon pull constantly on Earth and everything on it, including the water in our oceans. Sometimes, when the Sun and Moon are pulling in approximately the same direction, tides can be very high. Where beaches slope gently down to the sea, the changing water level can be very obvious.

High tide

Low tide

The phases of the Moon

Why does the Moon change shape?

Over a period of about four weeks, the Moon's shape in the night sky goes through a regular series of changes. These shapes are called the phases of the Moon. In fact, half of the Moon is constantly illuminated by the Sun (shown in the inner circle). However, as the Moon moves around the Earth, we see different parts of that illuminated half (outer circle).

Last quarter

Crescent

Waning gibbous

Sunlight

Full Moon

Earth

Crescent

Waxing gibbous

First quarter

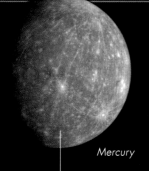

Mercury

Mercury's surface is covered in craters

What is the smallest planet?

A The smallest planet is Mercury: It is about 3,000 miles (4,900 km) across, which is only 38 percent the size of Earth (the largest of the rocky planets). Mercury turns slowly on its axis, which means days there last 88 times as long as days on Earth.

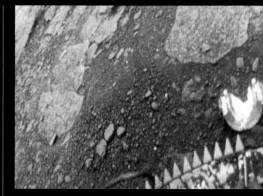

Surface of Venus

Venus has such a thick, cloudy atmosphere that its surface cannot be seen

Venus

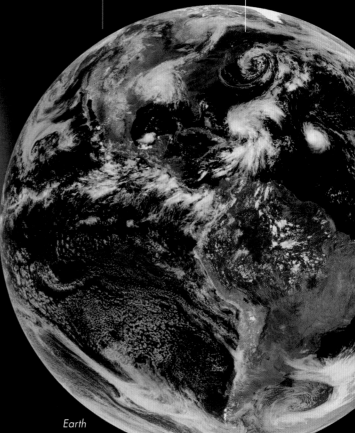

Earth is the densest planet in the Solar System

Earth

What are the rocky planets?

The rocky planets are the four closest to the Sun: Mercury, Venus, Earth, and Mars. All have rocky surfaces and outer layers, with metallic cores deep inside. They are also sometimes called the terrestrial (meaning Earthlike) or inner planets. Compared to the giant planets farther from the Sun, they are all small and dense. They take much less time to travel around the Sun and are warmer because they are closer to the Sun.

Q What is Earth made of ?

A Earth is made primarily of iron. This metal, together with nickel and others, forms the core of our planet. Thick layers of rock, which are mainly composed of oxygen, silicon, and magnesium, surround the core. Earth's atmosphere is mostly nitrogen, with some oxygen and other gases.

Are Earth and Venus similar planets?

Although almost identical in size and composition, Venus is very different from Earth. Venus is a lifeless, desertlike planet where the sky is yellow, as can be seen in this picture taken by the *Venera 14* space probe, and always cloudy. Venus is far hotter than Earth, partly because it is closer to the Sun and partly because its atmosphere traps much more heat.

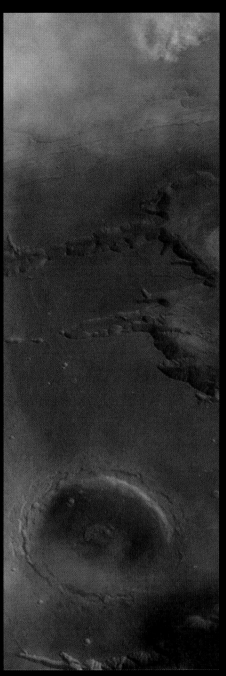

The reddish color of Mars is caused by the presence of rust in its sandy soil

Mars

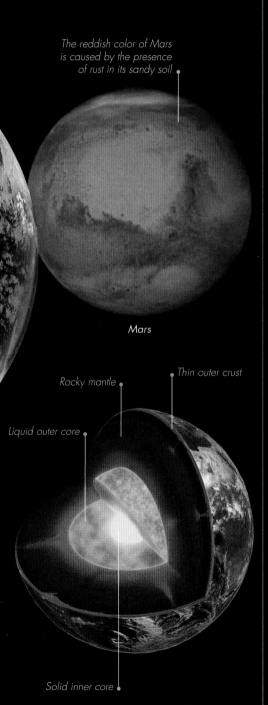

Thin outer crust

Rocky mantle

Liquid outer core

Solid inner core

Cross section of Earth

Dust storm on Mars

What is the weather like on Mars?

On Mars, the atmosphere is more than 100 times thinner than on Earth. This means that on Mars there can be no strong winds or rain, but snow sometimes falls there. On average, Mars is much colder than Earth, and parts of the planet are often frosty. There are sometimes dust storms on Mars, which can be big enough to cover the whole planet. Like Earth, Mars has ice caps around its poles. They contain solid carbon dioxide as well as water ice.

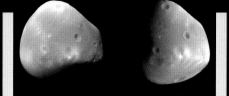

Phobos and Deimos

More Facts

- Mars has two tiny moons called Phobos and Deimos (Greek for fear and terror).

- Venus spins backward compared to Earth and most of the other planets.

- More than 75 percent of Earth is covered in water, and it is the only known planet to support life.

- Mercury has almost no atmosphere at all, so it has no real weather. Every day is scorching hot and every night is colder than anywhere on Earth.

Has there ever been life on Mars?

Millions of years ago, Mars had a much thicker atmosphere than it does today, and water flowed across its surface. It is possible that life may have existed on the planet under these conditions. If it did, it was probably more like germs than the creatures in science fiction films.

Science fiction illustration of Martian life

Q Which is the biggest planet?

A Jupiter is the biggest planet, with a width of more than 82,000 miles (133,000 km). It is large enough for 1,300 objects the size of Earth to fit inside it. This planet is also the most massive world in the Solar System—2.5 times the total mass of all the other planets. Jupiter is almost as large as it is possible for a planet to be. Adding much more mass would make Jupiter smaller because its gravity would increase and pull it into a smaller volume.

Saturn's rings may be rubble from a destroyed moon, or made of material left over from the formation of the Solar System

Size of Earth in relation to the giant planets

The white ovals are cool storm-cloud systems

Jupiter

The Great Red Spot is a storm that has lasted for more than three centuries

Why are the giant planets so big?

Jupiter, Saturn, Uranus, and Neptune formed in parts of the Solar System where there were plentiful supplies of hydrogen and helium. Once these planets began to form, their gravity pulled in more and more of these materials, allowing them to grow to huge sizes. All the giant planets move slowly around the Sun, which means they have very long years—a year on Jupiter is longer than 11 Earth-years, while a year on Neptune is nearly 165 Earth-years.

More Facts

- All the giant planets have deep, very cold atmospheres, and many moons.

- Jupiter has the largest family of moons in the Solar System, with at least 63 known moons.

- Io, one of Jupiter's moons, has many active volcanoes on its surface caused by the effects of Jupiter's gravity.

- Saturn is so light that it would float on water.

Which planets have rings?

Q **A** All the giant planets have rings. Saturn's rings are the brightest, and made of a vast number of ice fragments. The rings of Jupiter and Uranus are made of dust, with the rings of Uranus being particularly dark. Neptune's rings are believed to be a mixture of ice and dust.

When was Uranus discovered?

Q **A** Uranus can just barely be seen with the naked eye, so it was observed many times by people who did not realize it was a planet. British astronomer William Herschel initially thought Uranus was a comet until he realized that it was a planet in 1781. Compared to other giant planets, Uranus has a fairly featureless appearance.

Why are Uranus and Neptune blue-green?

Q **A** Both Uranus and Neptune contain the gas methane in their deep atmospheres, which gives them their blue-green color. Scientists are unsure why Neptune is a more intense blue than Uranus, since they contain about the same amount of methane. Hurricanes can sometimes be seen on Neptune as huge dark spots.

Uranus generates less internal heat than other giant planets, so its atmosphere is less disturbed

• Great Dark Spot—about the size of Earth—was a short-lived storm

Uranus

Neptune

Saturn

• Saturn's atmosphere consists mainly of hydrogen

Which is the largest moon in the Solar System?

Q **A** Jupiter's moon Ganymede is the largest in the Solar System. It is mainly made of rock and ice, and it is thought to contain an enormous underground ocean. Although Ganymede is larger than the planet Mercury, it is less than half as massive. As Ganymede orbits Jupiter, it turns so that the same part of the moon always faces the planet.

Ganymede

■ Uranus spins on its side. This means that night on some parts of the planet can last more than 40 Earth-years.

■ Triton, one of Neptune's moons, has geysers made of liquid nitrogen.

Artist's impression of Triton

Pluto is so far away that the Sun is tiny, dim, and cold

Pluto used to be classified as a planet

Artist's impression of Pluto from one of its moons

What are asteroids?

Asteroids are tiny worlds made of rock, metal, or a mixture of the two. Most are found between the orbits of Mars and Jupiter in an area called the Asteroid Belt. The majority are thought to be rubble left over from the formation of the planets; others may be the broken fragments of larger worlds. A few asteroids are hundreds of miles across, but most are much smaller. Some asteroids have their own tiny moons, and a few have been visited by spacecraft from Earth.

What is a dwarf planet?

A dwarf planet is a small round world in orbit around the Sun. So far, astronomers have identified five, including Pluto. Four of them are part of the Kuiper Belt, an area beyond Neptune containing lumps of rocky material left over from the formation of the Solar System. The fifth dwarf planet, Ceres, is in the Asteroid Belt.

The outer edge of the Oort Cloud may be nearly a light year from the Sun

Sun

Where do comets come from?

Beyond the Kuiper Belt is the Oort Cloud, a huge round swarm of icy objects stretching trillions of miles into space. Sometimes, objects from the belt or cloud are nudged by the gravity of passing stars and start to fall toward the Sun on long oval orbits. They are then referred to as comets. Many meteoroids are the remains of old comets.

Comet Hale-Bopp

What is a comet?

A comet is a huge lump of ice and rock, similar to an enormous dirty snowball. As the comet moves through the inner Solar System, the increasing heat of the Sun "boils" the ice, which streams away from the Sun in the form of a tail. A second tail, made of dust, also forms. These tails make comets much more visible—sometimes they can be seen with the naked eye in the night sky.

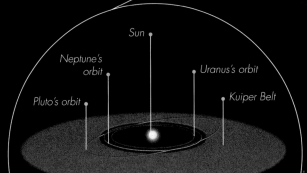

Sun

Neptune's orbit

Uranus's orbit

Pluto's orbit

Kuiper Belt

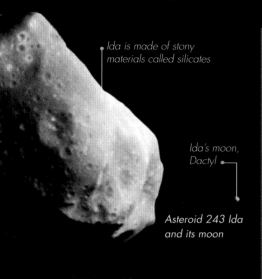

Ida is made of stony
materials called silicates

Ida's moon,
Dactyl

Asteroid 243 Ida
and its moon

Q/A What is a shooting star?

A shooting star, also known as a meteor, is a streak of light in the sky caused by a rocky or metallic object from space (called a meteoroid) burning up as it falls through Earth's atmosphere. Sometimes, if the falling object is large enough, it will not completely burn up in the atmosphere and a fragment will fall to Earth. This leftover piece of space material is then called a meteorite. Meteor showers are named after the constellation in which they appear: The Leonids, for instance, appear in the constellation of Leo every November.

Meteors during a Leonid meteor shower

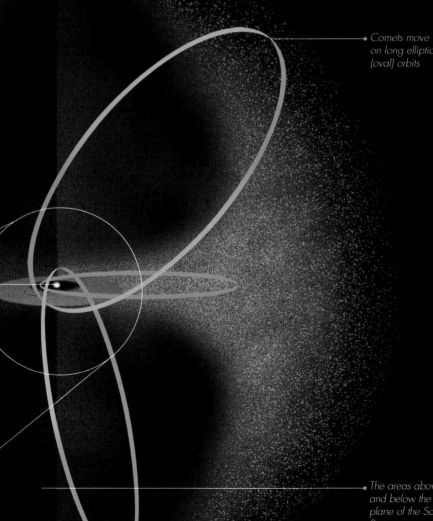

Comets move
on long elliptical
(oval) orbits

The areas above
and below the
plane of the Solar
System are
almost empty

Some comets take
many thousands of
years to complete
a single orbit

More Facts

■ The Hoba meteorite in Namibia is the largest known. Made of iron, it weighs more than 60 tons.

■ More meteorites are found in parts of Antarctica, where they were trapped in the ice when they fell, than anywhere else on Earth.

■ A tektite is a lump of black or very dark-green glass formed when a meteorite strikes the Earth.

■ The dinosaurs are thought to have died out following the impact of an asteroid or comet, which raised up such vast amounts of dust that the Sun's light was blocked out for many months, cooling the Earth's climate so much that they could not survive.

Artist's impression of a comet impact

DEEP SPACE

Whirlpool Galaxy

What is a galaxy?

A galaxy is a huge spinning group of stars, held together by gravity. It is known that, in addition to the stars that we can see, all galaxies also contain a great deal of dark matter that we cannot. It is thought that most of the stars in the Universe are members of a galaxy. Most galaxies probably have supermassive black holes at their centers.

Map of the Milky Way

Q **Which galaxy is ours?**

A Our own galaxy is called the Milky Way. Part of it can be seen on dark, moonless nights when there are no clouds, appearing as a long streak of patchy light curving across the sky. The bright central region of the Milky Way, where stars and nebulae are most concentrated, is in a part of the sky best seen from southern countries.

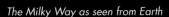

The Milky Way as seen from Earth

Q **What part of the Milky Way do we live in?**

A The Milky Way has several bright starry arms (people disagree over the exact number). The Solar System is in one of these arms, called the Orion Arm because the part that is visible from Earth lies in the constellation of Orion. The region of the arm that we live in is called the Local Spur.

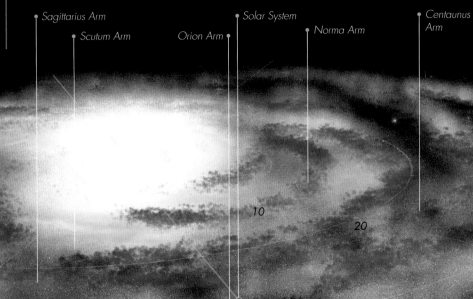

Sagittarius Arm

Scutum Arm

Orion Arm

Solar System

Norma Arm

Centaunus Arm

Carina Arm

10

20

30

40

Thousands of light years from center

Central bulge contains a dense core of older stars

Galactic disk contains young stars and large quantities of dust and gas

Solar System

Side-on view of the Milky Way

Q How big is the Milky Way?

A The Milky Way contains about 100 billion to 400 billion stars and its total mass is between 600 billion and 1 trillion times that of the Sun. The Milky Way is shaped like a thin discus, about 1 billion light years thick and 100,000 light years across. About 90 percent of the mass of the Milky Way is in the form of dark matter.

M82, a nearby starburst galaxy

Q What is a starburst galaxy?

A A starburst galaxy is one in which many stars are being born at about the same time. This often happens when a galaxy passes by, or through, another galaxy: The changing gravitational forces trigger the collapse of gas clouds from which stars are born. In order to become a starburst galaxy, a galaxy needs a plentiful supply of gas, from which stars can be made. By studying nearby starburst galaxies, astronomers can learn more about the processes that formed our own Sun.

More Facts

- The word *galaxy* comes from the Greek word for milky, because the Milky Way looks like a stream of milk in the sky.

- It takes about 250 million years for the Sun to make one orbit around the center of the Milky Way.

- There is a ring of stars around our galaxy called the Monoceros Ring. The stars may have been pulled from a nearby dwarf galaxy.

- Astronomer William Herschel was the first person to try to make a map of the Milky Way, which he completed in the 1700s. However, it was much too small because he didn't realize that many of the Milky Way's stars are hidden from us by dust clouds.

William Herschel

Large Magellanic Cloud

Q What are the Magellanic Clouds?

A The Magellanic Clouds are two small galaxies that orbit the Milky Way. The Large Magellanic Cloud is about 160,000 light years from us and the Small Magellanic Cloud is about 200,000 light years away. They can be seen only from the Southern Hemisphere and they are named after Ferdinand Magellan, a Portuguese explorer who was one of the first Europeans to see them in 1519.

What is the Local Group?

The Local Group is the cluster of galaxies of which our own Milky Way is a member. It contains about thirty other galaxies and stretches for about 10 million light years through space. It has a mass about a trillion times greater than the Sun's. Most of the other galaxies in the Local Group are much smaller and dimmer than the Milky Way and many of these small galaxies are in orbit around the larger ones.

Q **Can we see the Local Group?**

A In addition to the Milky Way, three galaxies in the group can be seen with the naked eye: the Andromeda Galaxy, the Large Magellanic Cloud, and the Small Magellanic Cloud. The Magellanic Clouds, however, can be seen only from the Southern Hemisphere.

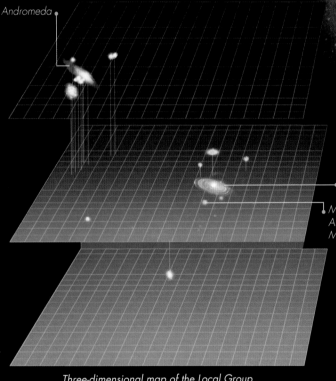

Andromeda

Milky Way

Most galaxies orbit Andromeda or the Milky Way

M110 is also an orbiting dwarf galaxy

Three-dimensional map of the Local Group

What are the largest galaxies in the Local Group?

The Andromeda Galaxy is the largest member of the Local Group and the Milky Way is the second largest. However, it is thought that the Milky Way may be the more massive of the two. The three largest galaxies are all spiral galaxies.

1 *The Andromeda Galaxy is about 290,000 light years across and contains about a trillion stars.*

2 *The Milky Way is about 100,000 light years across. It contains fewer stars than Andromeda but more dark matter.*

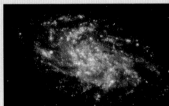

3 *Triangulum is about 50,000 light years across. It is thought that it may be in orbit around the Andromeda Galaxy.*

What is a supercluster?

Superclusters are collections of groups and clusters of galaxies, which are shaped like long, thin strands, hundreds of millions of light years in length. The Local Group is part of the Virgo Supercluster, which gets its name from the Virgo Cluster, its largest cluster of galaxies.

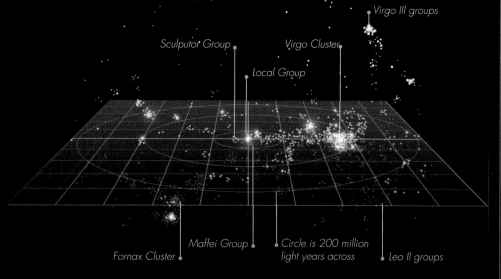

Virgo III groups

Sculptor Group

Virgo Cluster

Local Group

The Virgo Supercluster

Fornax Cluster

Maffei Group

Circle is 200 million light years across

Leo II groups

M32, a dwarf galaxy that orbits Andromeda

What is a filament?

Superclusters are grouped into filaments, which are thought to be the largest structures of all, hundreds of millions of light years in length. The filamentary structure of the Universe was probably set very soon after the Big Bang. Superclusters then formed within the filaments, through the action of gravity, over billions of years. This filament is called the Sloan Great Wall, and is nearly 1.5 billion light years long, and about 1 billion light years from Earth. The filament to which the Milky Way belongs is called the Pisces-Cetus Supercluster Complex.

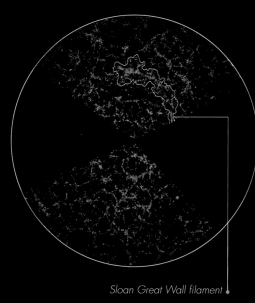

Sloan Great Wall filament

Andromeda

4 At 20,000 light years across, the Large Magellanic Cloud is the fourth largest galaxy in the Local Group.

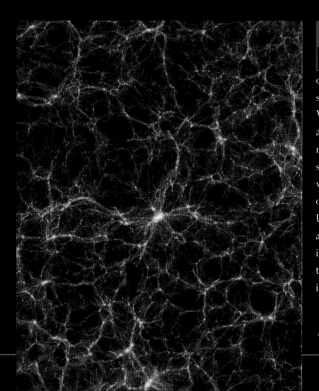

What are supervoids?

Voids are the vast dark empty spaces that separate the filaments of the Universe. They contain very few stars or galaxies—perhaps none at all. Voids are tens of millions of light years across. The largest voids, hundreds of millions of light years in size, are sometimes called supervoids. This picture was produced from a mathematical model of the evolution of a huge area of the Universe, more than 2 billion light years across. There are about 20 million galaxies in the model, and the image shows that these galaxies have arranged themselves in filaments, with voids in between.

Filaments and voids

What shapes are galaxies?

Galaxies are grouped by shape into four main types: spirals, ellipticals, irregulars, and lenticulars. In 1936, American astronomer Edwin Hubble classified galaxies according to their shapes, and his system is often used by astronomers today.

1 Spirals are thin and flat, with arms and a central bulge. The arms are home to new stars, while older stars reside in the bulge.

2 Elliptical galaxies vary in shape from spheres to disks. About 1 in 10 known galaxies are of this type.

3 A lenticular galaxy looks like a cross between a spiral and an elliptical galaxy. Like ellipticals, they form few new stars.

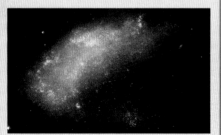

4 All other galaxies are referred to as irregulars. They are rich in gas and dust and contain many star-forming regions.

How many galaxies are there?

There are more than 100 billion galaxies in the known Universe. Each galaxy consists of millions of stars and clouds of dust and gas, kept in place by gravity. Galaxies began to form billions of years ago, shortly after the Universe was born. Pulled by gravity, matter clumped together to make large groups of massive stars. Many of the large galaxies that astronomers can see have formed from the merging together of smaller ones.

Circinus Galaxy

Q A How big is a galaxy?

The smallest galaxies, like Circinus, are known as dwarfs. The smallest dwarfs contain a few million stars, and the largest have a few billion. Dwarf galaxies are common in the Universe — the Milky Way has more than a dozen of them in orbit around it. Some of the largest galaxies, called giant ellipticals, are found at the centers of galaxy clusters.

Q A What are the Mice?

Named after their long tails and small bodies, the Mice are a pair of galaxies that are colliding with each other. Most of the stars in galaxies are a long way apart, so when galaxies collide there is little chance of stars crashing into one another. But the gravity of each galaxy sets off star formation in the other, and the shapes of both galaxies will be changed by the collision.

The Mice

Central region of our galaxy • Center

Q What is in the center of our galaxy?

A In the center of our galaxy there is a supermassive black hole, which has a mass millions of times greater than the Sun's. Although it cannot be seen directly, we know it is there because its enormous gravitational pull affects the motion of stars close to it. By combining X-ray and infrared images, we can peer through the dust clouds that hide the center of our galaxy.

Q Why are galaxies dusty?

A It is thought that the dust seen in many galaxies is produced in the atmospheres of red giants and other ancient stars. The Sombrero Galaxy has a thick ring of dust around it, and our own galaxy also contains many dust clouds; the dust particles that make up these regions are usually either like tiny pieces of soot or very fine sand.

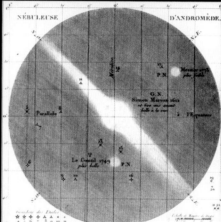

Charles Messier's sketch of Andromeda

More Facts

■ The Andromeda Galaxy is often referred to as M31, because it was the thirty-first entry in French astronomer Charles Messier's catalog. Messier published his list of what we now know to be deep-sky objects in 1774.

■ In the future, our galaxy will probably collide with the Andromeda Galaxy. Although the two are rushing together at a speed of more than 60 miles (100 km) per second, it will be more than 4 billion years before they collide.

■ The largest known galaxy is called IC 1101; it is about 5 million light years across, which is many times larger than the Milky Way. IC 1101 also contains more than a hundred times as many stars as our own galaxy.

Sombrero Galaxy

Are there clouds in space?

Even with the naked eye, several cloudy shapes can be seen in the night sky, and many more can be observed through telescopes. Some are bright and some are dark, but all are called nebulae, from the Latin word for clouds. Many nebulae are named after the things that they resemble, such as the Butterfly Nebula, the Ant Nebula, and the Little Ghost Nebula.

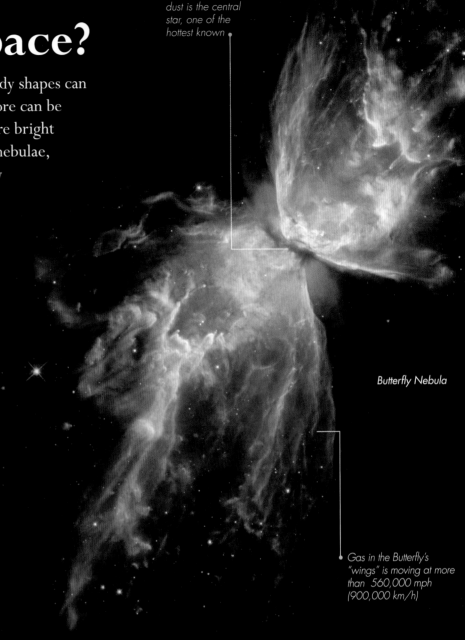

Hidden behind a thick cloud of dust is the central star, one of the hottest known

Butterfly Nebula

Gas in the Butterfly's "wings" is moving at more than 560,000 mph (900,000 km/h)

Q Where did the Crab Nebula come from?

A The Crab Nebula is the remains of a star that was seen exploding in 1054 CE. Chinese and Arabian astronomers saw it and watched its brightness fade for more than a year. Although the explosion was long before 1054 CE, its light took more than 6,000 years to reach Earth. The explosion that created the nebula left behind a pulsar—a spinning star that sends beams of radio waves sweeping across Earth.

Q Why is the Orion Nebula studied so often?

A On a dark, clear, moonless night the Orion Nebula can be seen with the naked eye as a patch of light in Orion's sword. The nebula is a region of space in which stars are being born. The distinctive red color of the nebula is caused by the presence of hydrogen gas, made to glow by very bright stars. Since the Orion Nebula is the closest large area of star-birth to Earth, it has been studied in great detail.

Crab Nebula

Orion Nebula

Q What is a dark nebula?

A Early astronomers thought that dark nebulae were starless holes in the Milky Way, but now we know that they are vast clouds of gas and dust that block out the light of stars behind them. This one, called Barnard 68, is about twice as massive as the Sun, and so large that if the Sun were at its center, all the planets would be inside it, too. In less than a million years, Barnard 68 will probably collapse to form a new star.

More Facts

- The Homunculus Nebula is a cloud of glowing gas thrown out by a pair of stars. It took about 170 years to reach its current shape. The gas is rushing outward at 1,500,000 mph (2,400,000 km/h).

- In 1774, French astronomer Charles Messier put together the first catalog of nebulae. He was interested in finding new comets, and since comets often look similar to nebulae, he used his catalog to make sure he didn't mix them up.

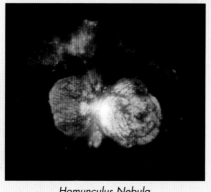

Homunculus Nebula

- Some objects that were once called nebulae are now known to be galaxies, such as the Andromeda Galaxy.

Barnard 68

Q How were the Pillars of Creation destroyed?

A The vast Pillars of Creation, which were several light years in length, once formed a part of the Eagle Nebula. They were the birthplace of many new stars. It is thought that the pillars themselves no longer exist, as a shock wave from a nearby exploding star was seen approaching them. The shock wave probably had enough power to sweep the pillars away. The pillars are still visible from Earth because we are seeing the light that left them before they were destroyed.

Pillars of Creation

• *Newborn stars forming*

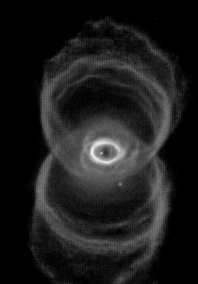

Hourglass Nebula

Q What is the Hourglass Nebula?

A The Hourglass is a planetary nebula. This type of nebula forms when stars shed their outer layers, leaving a tiny white dwarf in the center. The white speck in the "eye" of the Hourglass Nebula is its white dwarf. The nebula's shape is caused by a "wind" of gas, which blows from the white dwarf and disturbs a cloud of glowing gas around it. The red color of the gas cloud shows that it contains nitrogen, while the central blue area gets its color from the presence of oxygen.

OTHER WORLDS

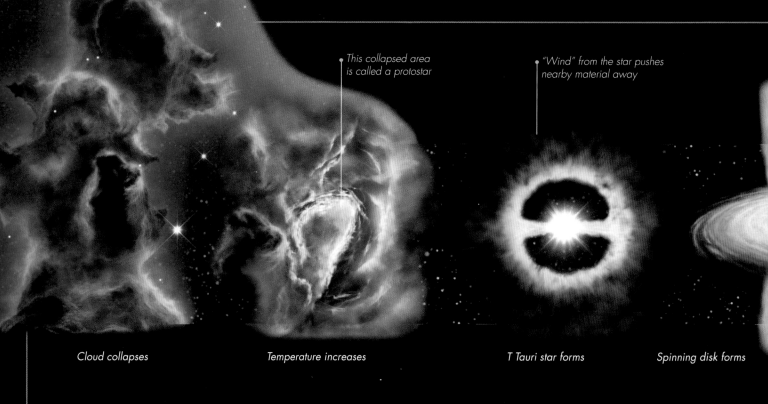

This collapsed area is called a protostar

"Wind" from the star pushes nearby material away

Cloud collapses   Temperature increases   T Tauri star forms   Spinning disk forms

Q | A — What is the biggest star?

The biggest star astronomers have found is VY Canis Majoris, which is between 1,800 and 2,100 times the diameter of the Sun (so a billion Sun-sized objects could fit inside it). It is also one of the brightest stars known, many thousands of times brighter than the Sun. It doesn't look bright in the night sky, because it is a long way from us—about 5,000 light years away.

Sun

VY Canis Majoris

How is a star born?

Stars are born in the hearts of dark clouds in space. They begin as clumps within the clouds, which collapse inward, pulled by gravity. This makes the compressed clumps of matter very hot—so hot that they begin to glow, and become T Tauri stars. These continue to get hotter, until nuclear reactions begin within their cores, turning the T Tauris into stars of other kinds, including stars like the Sun.

Q | A — What are the different types of star clusters?

A star cluster is a group of stars that are close together in space, usually because they have formed from the same cloud. Globular clusters are round, with many stars packed closely together. Open clusters contain fewer stars, which are more spread out. Globular clusters are found in orbit around the central parts of galaxies, including our own.

Some globular clusters have black holes at their centers

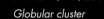

Globular cluster

Powerful winds throw out more material

Solid particles and clumps start to appear

Young planets grow as they sweep up material from the disk

The central star is similar to our Sun

Sunlike star forms

Planets begin to form

Central star

Albireo, a double star

More Facts

- Many stars, including the Sun, have spots on their surfaces—sometimes enormous ones. Spots are cooler areas. They are caused by powerful magnetic fields.

- When the Sun was a T Tauri star, it was brighter than it is today because its mass was spread over a larger area, so it had a larger shining surface.

- In the past, people suggested names for several new constellations, which did not prove popular, including Latin versions of the Printing Office and the Slug.

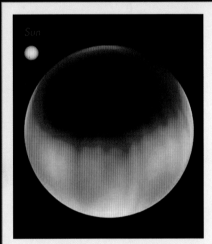

HD 12545, a spotted star

Q A What is a double star?

A double star is a pair of stars that are very close together in the sky. In some cases this is because they are close together in space, too, but in others they are not—they just happen to lie in the same direction from us. The brightest star in Albireo is itself a double, though the stars are so close they are hard to see separately.

What is a constellation?

A constellation is a pattern of stars in the sky, named after an object, a mythological person, or a creature. All the stars near the pattern are also members of the constellation. The sky is grouped into 88 constellations, helping stargazers find their way around the night sky.

1 This is how the constellation Orion looks in the sky.

2 Orion's bright stars can be linked to create an imaginary pattern.

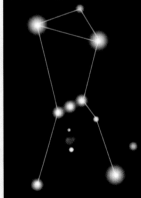

3 The figure represents Orion the great hunter. In Greek mythology, he was the son of Poseidon, the mighty sea god.

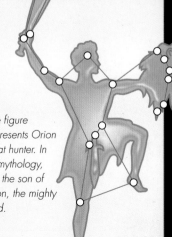

Do stars explode?

There are many types of exploding stars. Most are actually pairs of stars: In some of them, material from one star is dragged to the other by the force of gravity until so much material is crushed together that nuclear explosions take place. In other cases, the explosion happens when the two stars actually merge together. These explosions are called novas or, if they are very bright, supernovas. Another type of supernova happens when massive stars run out of fuel and collapse. Again, it is the crush of material that causes the explosion.

Cassiopeia A, remnant of a supernova explosion

Q **What is a red giant?**

A The Sun, like other stars of about the same mass, will turn into a red giant one day. After billions of years, such stars run out of hydrogen to use as fuel and start to use a new fuel, helium. This makes the stars burn brighter and they become much larger, while their color becomes redder. The red giant part of a star's life lasts only a few million years.

Red giants throw off shells of gas, which turn to dust and drift out into space

Blue and orange stars in double star clusters NGC 884 and NGC 869

Q **Are the stars different colors?**

A In the night sky, the stars look white because they are so faint: Our eyes can't see colors unless there is plenty of light. Through a telescope, the true colors of stars can be more easily seen: There are red, orange, and yellow stars as well as pink, white, and blue ones. Usually, redder stars are cooler, though sometimes their light is reddened because of the space dust it passes through.

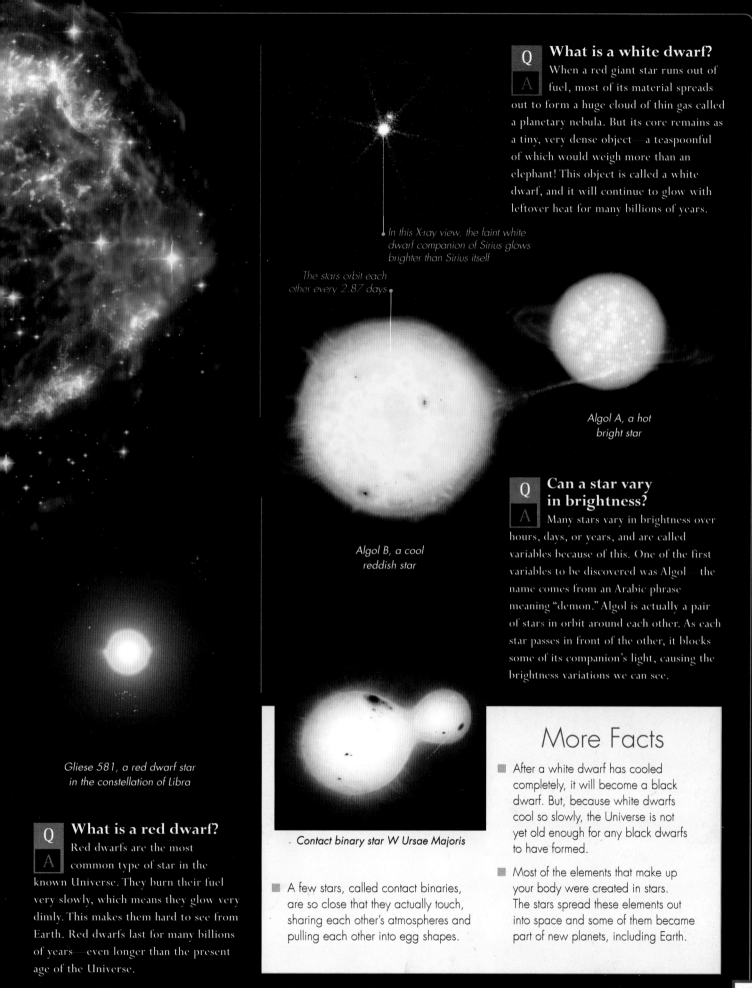

What is a white dwarf?

When a red giant star runs out of fuel, most of its material spreads out to form a huge cloud of thin gas called a planetary nebula. But its core remains as a tiny, very dense object—a teaspoonful of which would weigh more than an elephant! This object is called a white dwarf, and it will continue to glow with leftover heat for many billions of years.

In this X-ray view, the faint white dwarf companion of Sirius glows brighter than Sirius itself

The stars orbit each other every 2.87 days

Algol A, a hot bright star

Algol B, a cool reddish star

Can a star vary in brightness?

Many stars vary in brightness over hours, days, or years, and are called variables because of this. One of the first variables to be discovered was Algol—the name comes from an Arabic phrase meaning "demon." Algol is actually a pair of stars in orbit around each other. As each star passes in front of the other, it blocks some of its companion's light, causing the brightness variations we can see.

Gliese 581, a red dwarf star in the constellation of Libra

What is a red dwarf?

Red dwarfs are the most common type of star in the known Universe. They burn their fuel very slowly, which means they glow very dimly. This makes them hard to see from Earth. Red dwarfs last for many billions of years—even longer than the present age of the Universe.

Contact binary star W Ursae Majoris

A few stars, called contact binaries, are so close that they actually touch, sharing each other's atmospheres and pulling each other into egg shapes.

More Facts

- After a white dwarf has cooled completely, it will become a black dwarf. But, because white dwarfs cool so slowly, the Universe is not yet old enough for any black dwarfs to have formed.

- Most of the elements that make up your body were created in stars. The stars spread these elements out into space and some of them became part of new planets, including Earth.

Why are black holes black?

The faster an object is thrown upward, the higher it rises. If it is thrown fast enough, it will never fall down again. It reaches what is called the escape velocity and escapes from Earth's gravity and continues on into space. Spacecraft that go to other planets have to reach this escape velocity. Where gravity is very strong, the escape velocity is so high that even light is too slow to escape. This makes objects with such strong gravity look black, and we call them black holes.

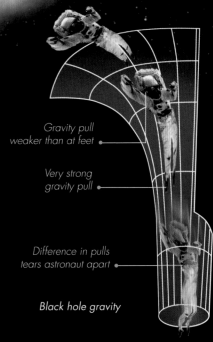

Gravity pull weaker than at feet

Very strong gravity pull

Difference in pulls tears astronaut apart

Black hole gravity

A gamma-ray burst

Q/A What would happen if you traveled to a black hole?

On Earth, you weigh a tiny bit less at the top of a mountain than at its base, because the top is a little farther from the center of the Earth, making the gravity pull slightly weaker there. If Earth were smaller but more massive, this change in gravity pull would be much larger. Very near a black hole, this effect is so large that the part of your body nearest to the hole would be pulled very much more strongly than the rest of you, so you would be pulled apart.

Q/A How do we know black holes exist?

Black holes can't be seen, but there are many facts that show us they exist. Matter that falls into them gives up some of its energy in the form of powerful radiation, which astronomers can detect in the form of X-rays. There are also sudden bursts of gamma rays (an even more powerful type of radiation) caused by a star collapsing and forming a new black hole.

Stephen Hawking

■ It used to be thought that black holes produced no radiation at all, but physicist Stephen Hawking showed that they are surrounded by a faint glow now called Hawking radiation.

More Facts

■ Although the idea of black holes was first suggested in 1783, it was not taken seriously until the work of Albert Einstein and other scientists in the 20th century proved they might exist.

■ The gravity of a black hole can sometimes act like a lens, causing the light from a more distant star to brighten for a short time. This effect is called gravitational lensing.

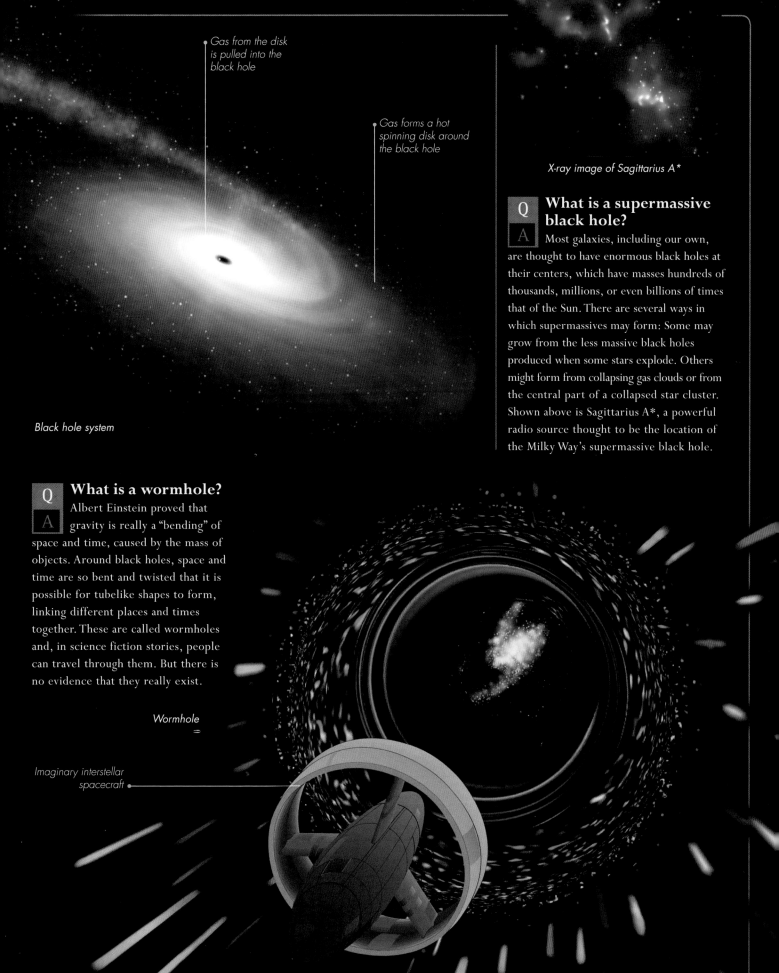

Gas from the disk
is pulled into the
black hole

Gas forms a hot
spinning disk around
the black hole

*X-ray image of Sagittarius A**

Black hole system

Q A What is a supermassive black hole?

Most galaxies, including our own, are thought to have enormous black holes at their centers, which have masses hundreds of thousands, millions, or even billions of times that of the Sun. There are several ways in which supermassives may form: Some may grow from the less massive black holes produced when some stars explode. Others might form from collapsing gas clouds or from the central part of a collapsed star cluster. Shown above is Sagittarius A*, a powerful radio source thought to be the location of the Milky Way's supermassive black hole.

Q A What is a wormhole?

Albert Einstein proved that gravity is really a "bending" of space and time, caused by the mass of objects. Around black holes, space and time are so bent and twisted that it is possible for tubelike shapes to form, linking different places and times together. These are called wormholes and, in science fiction stories, people can travel through them. But there is no evidence that they really exist.

Wormhole

Imaginary interstellar
spacecraft

Artist's impression of an alien world

Are we alone?

Spacecraft have explored the Solar System and found no life beyond Earth, and there is no evidence for life outside the Solar System either. However, life on Earth developed from a mixture of simple chemicals. If similar chemicals and conditions existed on another Earthlike planet, there is no reason to think that living things would not appear there, too. Since the Universe is so vast, it seems very likely that many such planets exist.

Q A Do other stars have planets?

So far, more than 1,100 planets have been found around other stars. The first such "exoplanet" was found in 1988, orbiting a star called Gamma Cephei, which is 45 light years from Earth. Most of these planets are much larger than Earth, but that is partly because larger planets are easier to find. Below, the Solar System is compared with the system of planets around 55 Cancri.

Q A Have postcards really been sent to aliens?

Several spacecraft that have been sent to explore the outer planets of our Solar System have carried "postcards"—special plaques and disks containing messages and images from Earth. Also, a number of radio messages have been sent from radio telescopes. The messages contain images of human beings and the Solar System.

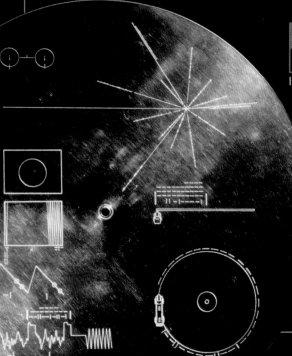

Cover of Voyager's recorded disk, including a map to show the location of the Solar System

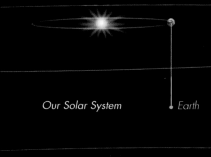

Our Solar System · *Earth*

How are exoplanets found?

A As a planet goes around a star, the star wobbles slightly. In some cases, this wobbling motion can be measured from Earth because it makes the light from the star change color very slightly. Also, sometimes an exoplanet passes across the face of the star it orbits and this blocks out a tiny fraction of the star's light. Very accurate measurements of starlight can detect this effect. The same thing happens in our own Solar System—Mercury and Venus occasionally pass across the face of the Sun, appearing as small dots.

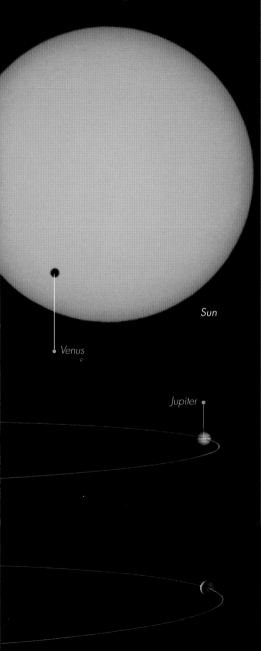

Sun

Venus

Jupiter

55 Cancri

Artist's impression of an alien spacecraft

What would aliens look like?

A Living things look the way they do because they have evolved to fit their environments—worms are just the right shape to burrow underground, while the bodies of glass squid are ideal for life in the deep sea. So, what aliens look like would depend on the conditions of the world they evolved on. It is likely that an alien planet would have many different environments on it, so its inhabitants would vary enormously, just as living things on our own world do.

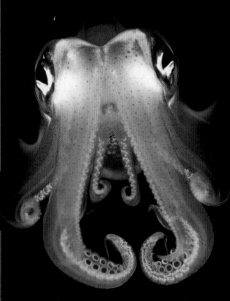

Glass squid

What are UFOs?

A UFO is short for unidentified flying object, and a great many of them have been sighted throughout the world. Although some people believe they are alien spacecraft, there is no good evidence for this, and most UFO sightings have been shown to be hoaxes or caused by meteors, weather balloons, planes, or unusual weather conditions. In 1947, there was a famous UFO sighting by Kenneth Arnold, a businessman, while he was flying his private plane in Washington State. Newspaper reports of his experience were followed by a huge increase in the number of reported UFOs.

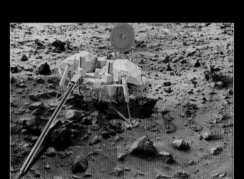

Viking lander on Mars

More Facts

■ The twin Viking landers reached Mars in 1977 to search for life on the planet. Their onboard laboratories reacted in an unexpected way to the chemicals they found in the soil, but it is not thought that this was because living things were present.

■ In 1977, a strange signal was detected by an American radio telescope: It could not be explained as any natural event. It is called the Wow! Signal because the astronomer who noticed it wrote "Wow!" on the computer printout.

■ In 1937, a radio broadcast of H.G. Wells's story *The War of the Worlds* made some people in the United States believe that an invasion from Mars was really taking place!

EXPLORING THE UNIVERSE

Gamma rays	X-rays	Ultraviolet rays	Infrared	Radio waves

Visible light

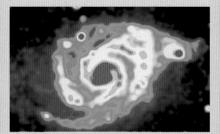

400   500   600   700   Wavelength (nanometers)

What do telescopes see?

This depends on the parts of the electromagnetic spectrum that the telescope is designed to detect. The images below show how the Whirlpool Galaxy looks when seen through different telescopes. The object to the right of the Whirlpool is another smaller galaxy.

1 *Radio waves pick out the magnetic fields of the Whirlpool. This image was made by the Very Large Array.*

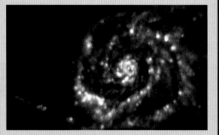

2 *Dusty areas and cooler stars are bright at infrared wavelengths, as shown by the Spitzer Space Telescope.*

3 *The Galaxy Evolution Explorer space telescope is sensitive to ultraviolet light, which is produced by the hottest stars.*

4 *Very hot gas, and the areas near black holes, produce X-rays. This image was produced by the Chandra X-ray space telescope.*

What do astronomers do?

Astronomers are scientists who study the Universe beyond Earth, and they do this in many ways. Theoretical astronomers invent theories about how the Universe, or things in it, formed or how they work. Using computers, they may make mathematical models based on their theories, and see if their models behave like the real thing. Observational astronomers use telescopes to study everything that can be detected in space, from cosmic dust grains to superclusters and filaments.

Very Large Array, New Mexico

Q What is electromagnetic radiation?

A Light can be thought of as being made of waves, and its colors as related to the lengths of those waves. In a rainbow, the colors are lined up in order of wavelength, from short violet waves to long red ones. Waves of shorter and longer lengths exist too, but we can't see them: Beyond red is infrared (which we can sometimes feel as heat) and then radio waves. Beyond violet are ultraviolet, X-rays, and gamma rays. Together, all these waves are known as electromagnetic radiation.

Chandra X-ray space telescope

Q What is the biggest telescope?

A The largest telescopes are radio telescopes—the biggest single dish (known as an antenna) is that of the Arecibo radio telescope in Puerto Rico, which is 1,001 ft (305 m) across. Shown below is the Very Large Array located in New Mexico. It consists of 27 antennae—each antenna measures 82 ft (25 m) across.

Separate antennae all point to the same part of the sky before combining their observations

Neutrino detectors in the Super-K

Q Why are there telescopes in old mines?

A Some telescopes detect things that are not part of the electromagnetic spectrum, including tiny particles called neutrinos, which travel through the Earth. Telescopes that detect them are built deep underground in old mines to shield them from the effects of electromagnetic radiation. Shown above is the Super-Kamiokande (or Super-K) telescope, built in a zinc mine, deep beneath a mountain in Japan.

Q What is a space telescope?

A A space telescope is a type of satellite. It orbits above Earth's atmosphere, so it can measure types of electromagnetic radiation that our air blocks out or weakens, including gamma rays, X-rays, ultraviolet, and infrared. Observations of visible wavelengths can be better from space too, with no clouds to get in the way or air movement to make the stars "twinkle."

More Facts

- Few professional astronomers actually look through their telescopes. Most use electronic devices called charge-coupled devices to capture images instead.

- To gather enough light to make pictures of faint objects like distant galaxies, telescopes sometimes point at the same spot in the sky for many hours—even days—at a time.

- The most recent nearby supernova was discovered by astronomers Ian Shelton and Oscar Duhalde at the Las Campanas Observatory in Chile, on February 24, 1987.

Ian Shelton at his telescope

Konstantin Tsiolkovsky

Q **Who invented the space rocket?**

A Russian scientist Konstantin Tsiolkovsky developed the first detailed theories of space-rocket flight, and published them in 1903. His mathematical study of the problem of escaping from the Earth's gravity showed that a multistage rocket would be needed to reach orbit. For most of his life, Tsiolkovsky's ideas were not taken very seriously, and it was many decades before they became a reality.

Yuri Gagarin

Q **Who was the first human in space?**

A The first human in space was Yuri Gagarin, a 27-year-old Russian pilot. He was blasted into space in 1961, in a spacecraft called *Swallow*. Gagarin was selected from twenty candidates partly because he was small enough to fit inside the cramped capsule.

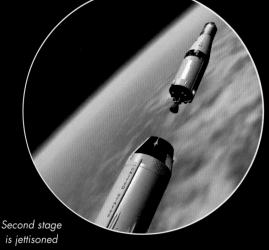

Second stage is jettisoned

How do spacecraft work?

To leave Earth, all spacecraft use rockets, which burn either solid or liquid fuel. The rockets carry oxygen with them, because fuel cannot burn without it. As they move up through the atmosphere, spacecraft leave their empty fuel tanks behind them. Once in space, some spacecraft use the gravity of other planets to change their direction of flight and speed them on their journeys. This Saturn V Moon rocket carried most of its fuel in stages, each of which was left behind once it was empty.

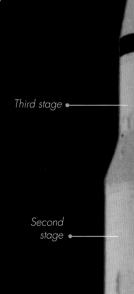

Apollo spacecraft

Third stage

Second stage

First stage

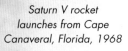

Saturn V rocket launches from Cape Canaveral, Florida, 1968

When did humans first reach the Moon?

The Soviet *Luna 2* spacecraft, the first human-made object to reach the Moon, crash-landed there in 1959. However, it was the American Apollo 11 mission that sent the first humans, Neil Armstrong and Buzz Aldrin, to the Moon's surface on July 20, 1969, with Armstrong being the first to set foot on the Moon.

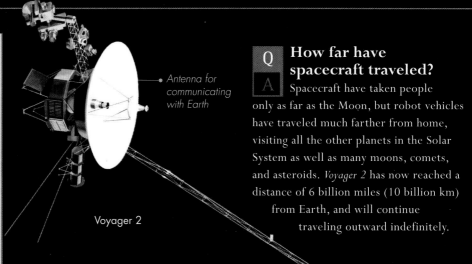

Antenna for communicating with Earth

Voyager 2

1 *The three-man crew boards the Saturn V rocket, carrying the Apollo capsule.*

2 *The crew touches down in an area called the Sea of Tranquility.*

3 *Astronaut Buzz Aldrin on the Moon—Neil Armstrong and the Apollo landing module are reflected in his visor.*

Q A How far have spacecraft traveled?

Spacecraft have taken people only as far as the Moon, but robot vehicles have traveled much farther from home, visiting all the other planets in the Solar System as well as many moons, comets, and asteroids. *Voyager 2* has now reached a distance of 6 billion miles (10 billion km) from Earth, and will continue traveling outward indefinitely.

More Facts

- ■ Earth's atmosphere gradually thins out with height, so there is no sudden beginning to space. However, 62 miles (100 km) above sea level is the official "edge" of space. The first rocket to reach this height was the V-2, a war rocket launched in 1942.

- ■ In the 1950s, a spacecraft was designed that would be pushed through space by nuclear bombs, one of which would explode every second.

- ■ In under ten seconds, a Saturn V rocket's stage 1 engines burn 30,000 gallons (110,000 liters) of fuel— enough to fill a swimming pool.

Postcard shows Laika, the first dog in space

- ■ The first space traveler was a dog named Laika, who traveled into space in 1957 in *Sputnik 2*, a Soviet spacecraft.

Q A Can anyone build a spacecraft?

Anyone with enough money can! *SpaceShipOne*, an experimental spacecraft that was launched in 2003, was entirely paid for by American billionaire Paul Allen, who worked with an aviation company to build it. More often though, it is the governments of rich countries, sometimes working together, that build spacecraft.

Part of the wing folds upward during descent to act as a brake

SpaceShipOne

The spacecraft is made of carbon fiber, a strong, light material

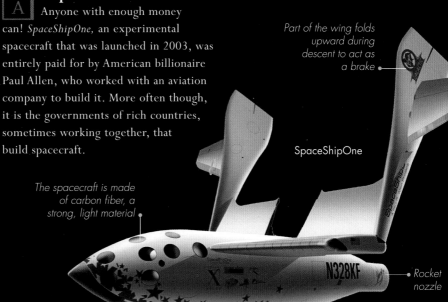

N328KF

Rocket nozzle

Primary life support
system supplying
oxygen, water, and
temperature control

Gloves have tethers to
hold tools, and one has
a built-in wristwatch

Secondary
oxygen pack

Suit is made
of 14 layers

Q **How do astronauts
walk in space?**

A When astronauts "walk" in space
they wear spacesuits called Extravehicular
Mobility Units to protect them from the
lack of air, dangerous radiation, and
extreme temperatures. They usually pull
themselves along their spacecraft, but they
also carry packs containing compressed gas:
By squirting the gas in one direction, the
astronaut moves through space in the other.

How many astronauts live on the ISS?

A crew of six astronauts live on the International Space Station
(ISS). They are replaced by a new crew every few months,
and while on board they carry out scientific research in the
weightless conditions there. The ISS is being built by the scientists
of 16 nations and has had people on board since 2000. It can
sometimes be seen in the night sky with the naked eye.
Astronauts travel to and from the ISS using American
and Russian spacecraft.

Soyuz 11

Salyut 1

Soyuz 11 *docking with the* Salyut 1,
June 7, 1971

Q **What was the first
space station?**

A The first space station was the
Soviet *Salyut 1*, which was launched in
1971. Its crews were launched separately,
in *Soyuz 10* and *Soyuz 11*. The *Soyuz 10*
crew was unable to dock with *Salyut*,
but the second crew successfully boarded
and remained there for 23 days. All three
crew members were killed on their way
back to Earth, when a valve accidentally
opened and the air in the cabin escaped.

International Space Station

Radiator rejects
excess heat

Radiator

Japanese
research
module

Astronauts aboard the ISS, April 2002

Q | What is it like living in a spacecraft?

A Space stations, and other objects in orbit, do not usually feel the pull of Earth's gravity and neither do people aboard them, which is why astronauts float. In these conditions, liquids drift around the cabin like bubbles, so drinks have to be sucked from containers. Astronauts need to attach their sleeping bags to the walls so they stay in one place while they sleep, and have to use specially designed toilets that suck away waste.

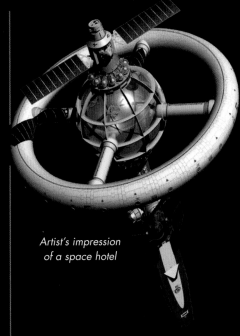

Artist's impression of a space hotel

Q | Could you book a vacation in space?

A You can take a trip to space if you can afford the ticket, which costs millions of dollars. For this price, you could travel up to the ISS in a Russian spacecraft. The first such space tourist was Dennis Tito, an American millionaire, who went on a space holiday in 2001. There are also plans to build space hotels in orbit later this century, where you could enjoy weightless conditions and amazing views of Earth and space.

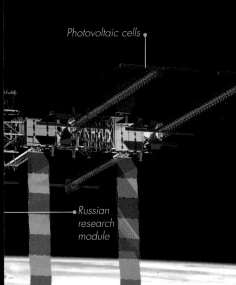

Photovoltaic cells produce electricity from sunlight

Photovoltaic cells

Russian research module

What are satellites?

A space station is just one kind of satellite (a satellite is an object that orbits another in space). There are currently more than 2,000 manmade satellites orbiting Earth, including some "dead" ones that will continue to orbit indefinitely. There are several kinds of satellites, each designed to do a particular job.

1 An early communications satellite, Syncom, was used to relay telephone conversations between distant parts of the world.

2 Cloudsat, a weather satellite, monitors cloud systems by radar, helping to investigate global warming.

3 This Global Positioning System (GPS) satellite helps people on Earth find their exact location.

4 RADARSAT-1 uses microwaves (short radio waves) to scan Earth, collecting data used to make maps and to study the land and sea.

Mysterious Universe

What is there left to discover?

In the last few hundred years, our understanding of the Universe has grown at an incredible rate, but the biggest questions of all remain unanswered: Why did the Universe begin? What is it made of? How will it end? There are also many mysteries concerning specific planets, stars, and galaxies, and great gaps in our knowledge of how such structures developed. But it seems certain that one day, science will explain it all.

NGC 4526

Q **A** ### What is dark energy?
Nearly three-quarters of the Universe is made of something we know almost nothing about: dark energy. In the 1990s, studies of distant supernovas showed that the expansion of the Universe is speeding up. Something—now called dark energy—must be working against gravity to push the parts of the Universe apart. The bright dot in galaxy NGC 4526 is a supernova, which provided evidence for dark energy.

Q **A** ### What is dark matter?
About a quarter of the Universe is made of dark matter. We know dark matter exists because of its gravitational effects on stars and starlight, but no one knows what it is. In this picture, the light from a distant cluster of galaxies is bent by an area of dark matter (artificially colored light blue) between the cluster and the Earth.

Cluster of galaxies in the constellation of Pisces

Jupiter

Q **A** ### Is there life on Europa?
Europa is one of Jupiter's moons, and it has a bitterly cold, icy surface. But deep under the ice, there is a great ocean, which is warmed by the effects of the gravity of Jupiter. It is possible that living things might exist in this ocean, as they do under similar conditions in the oceans of Earth. One day, a robot spacecraft from Earth may go to Europa, to dig down through the ice to investigate.

Artist's impression of Europa's icy surface

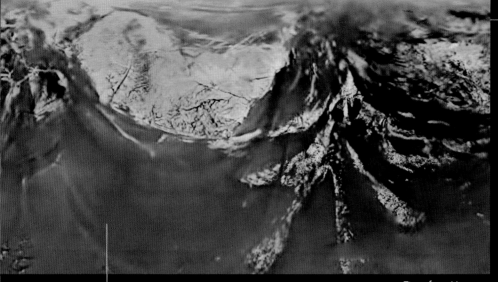

*Dark plain was
flooded in the past*

Titan from Huygens

What is hidden on Titan?

A Titan is the largest moon of Saturn, with an atmosphere so murky that the moon's surface was a mystery until it was photographed by the Cassini mission in 2005. Together, the *Cassini* orbiter and the *Huygens* probe discovered a landscape of hills, and strange seas of ethane and methane. In 2010, it was suggested by some scientists that unusual chemical changes in the atmosphere could be caused by living creatures.

*Area rich in
dark matter*

*Arecibo's dish is
built into a natural
depression*

Arecibo radio telescope

How can I help hunt for aliens?

A Since 1999, astronomers searching for alien signals have used a special receiver at the Arecibo radio telescope in Puerto Rico to collect an enormous amount of data from space. Chunks of this data are sent, via the Internet, to a worldwide network of home computers, which search for messages in the data. You can join the hunt by going to the SETI@home website.

More Facts

Epsilon Aurigae system

■ Epsilon Aurigae is a star that, about every 27 years, becomes dim. Astronomers know that this happens because the star passes behind something that it is orbiting—but they don't know what this huge, dark object is.

■ For unknown reasons, Neptune radiates more than twice as much heat as it receives from the Sun.

■ Since the 1960s, intense bursts of gamma rays have been detected from deep space. One type of burst is known to be caused by the destruction of stars, but the source of the others is a mystery.

■ In the 2000s, it was discovered that clusters of galaxies seem to be moving together in the same direction—a phenomenon called dark flow, which has not yet been fully explained.

INDEX

CREDITS

The publisher would like to thank Polly Boyd for proofreading and Jackie Brind for the index.

The publisher would like to thank the following for their kind permission to reproduce their photographs: (**Key:** a-above; b-below/bottom; c-center; l-left; r-right; t-top)

The Advertising Archives: 25br; **Alamy Images:** Ulrich Baumgarten/vario images GmbH & Co. KG 46bc; **Chandra X-Ray Observatory:** NASA/CXC/A. Siemiginowska (CfA)/J. Bechtold(U. Arizona) 13crb; NASA/JPL-Caltech 52clb; NRAO/AUI/NSF 52cla; X-ray: NASA/CXC/Wesleyan Univ./R. Kilgard et al; UV: NASA/JPL-Caltech; Optical: NASA ESA/S. Beckwith & Hubble Heritage Team (STScI/AURA); IR: NASA/JPL-Caltech/Univ. of AZ/R. Kennicutt 52bl; X-ray: NASA/CXC/UMass/D. Wang et al./Optical: NASA/ESA/STScI/D. Wang et al./IR: NASA/JPL-Caltech/SSC/S.Stolovy 37tc; **Corbis:** Michael Benson/Kinetikon Pictures/Encyclopedia 20bc; Bettmann 11br, 22tl, 28-29tc; Daniel J. Cox/Latitude 21c; Dennis di Cicco/Latitude 28clb; The Gallery Collection 15bc (Galileo); Tony Hallas/Science Faction 4bl, 29tr, 34-35c; NASA-digital version copyright/Science Faction 6-7bc, 14-15bc, 56-57bc; NASA/Encyclopedia 5cb; NASA/EPA 45clb; NASA/Roger Ressmeyer 39cr, 53tr; NASA/Science Faction 30-31, 57tr; NASA, H. Ford (JHU), G. Illingworth (UCSC/LO), M. Clampin (STScI), G. Hartig (STScI), the ACS Science Team, and ESA: Hubble/STScI/NASA 36br; Louie Psihoyos/Science Factio/Terra 59cr; William Radcliffe/Science Faction 5br, 6clb, 26-27c; Otto Rogge/Flirt 58tl; Chuck Savage/Surf 14fcl; Denis Scott/Comet 28tl; Space Telescope Wide Field and Planetary Camera 2/Bettman 39bl; Stocktrek Images/Frank Hettick/Stocktrek Images/Alloy 58-59bl; STScI/NASA 21crb; Visuals Unlimited/Encyclopedia 36tl, 38br; Bobby Yip/

Reuters 49cl; T. **Credner, Allthesky.com:** 15br; **Dorling Kindersley:** NASA 23tc, 24cr; Satellite Imagemap (c) 1996-2003 Planetary Visions 25bl; **Dreamstime.com:** Don Stevenson/Azpworldwide 62-63; **ESA:** CNES/Arianespace-Optique vidéo du CSG 50-51; Hubble 46-47tc; Eckhard Slawik 35bl; **European Southern Observatory (ESO):** A. Roquette 46cl; **FLPA:** Chris Newbert/Minden Pictures 49bc; **Getty Images:** Aaron Foster 49tc; GSO Images/The Image Bank 17br; Jean-Leon Huens/National Geographic 12cb; Joe McNally 52-53bc; NASA 38bl; NASA/ESA/Hubble SM4 ERO Team 38cra; NASA/Getty Images News 56tl; Joe Raedle 21tr; Rolls Press/Popperfoto 54clb; Space Frontiers/Archive Photos 33bc; Stocktrek Images 32tl, 36cla, 37bl; **NASA and The Hubble Heritage Team (AURA/STScI):** High-Z Supernova Search Team 58cla; NASA/Andrew S. Wilson (University of Maryland)/Patrick L. Shopbell (Caltech)/Chris Simpson (Subaru Telescope)/Thaisa Storchi-Bergmann and F. K. B. Barbosa (UFRGS, Brazil)/and Martin J. Ward (University of Leicester, U.K.) 36-37c; NASA/ESA/A. Sarajedini (University of Florida) and G. Piotto (University of Padua [Padova]) 42br; NASA/ESA/M. J. Jee and H. Ford (Johns Hopkins University) 4-5 (background), 6-7 (background), 58-59c, 60-61; NASA/ESA/R. Windhorst (Arizona State University), P. McCarthy (Carnegie Institution of Washington), STScI-PRC10-01a 15cra; NASA/ESA/the Hubble Heritage Team (STScI/AURA), J. Bell (Cornell University), and M. Wolff (Space Science Institute, Boulder) 25cl; NASA / ESA/The Hubble Heritage Team (STScI/AURA)/W. Keel (University of Alabama, Tuscaloosa) 36clb; NASA/ESA/The Hubble Heritage Team (STScI/AURA) M. Gregg (Univ. Calif.-Davis and Inst. for Geophysics and Planetary Physics, Lawrence Livermore Natl. Lab.) 36bl; NASA/ESA/the Hubble SM4 ERO Team 39tr; **Courtesy of JAXA:** 44br; **NASA:** 6tl, 53tc, 55bl, 55cla, 55clb; CXC/Caltech/M. Muno et al. 47tr; ESA/JPL/University of Arizona 59tl; ESA/The Hubble Heritage Team/(STScI/AURA) M. Mountain (STScI)/P. Puxley (NSF)/J. Gallagher (U.

Wisconsin) 33cl; ESA/R. Windhorst (Arizona State University)/H. Yan (Spitzer Science Center, Caltech) 10tr; Glenn Image Gallery 47tl; Johns Hopkins University Applied Physics Laboratory/Arizona State University/Carnegie Institution of Washington 24tl; JPL 14c (Planet Earth), 18-19, 27br, 48bl, 48-49bc; JPL/Arizona State University 16bl; JPL/Mosaic by Mattias Malmer 4tl, 24cl; JPL/MSSS 25ca; JPL-Caltech 34br; JPL-Caltech/R. Hurt/SSC/Caltech 34bc (Milky Way); JPL-Caltech/R. Kennicutt (Univ. of Arizona)/DSS 52tl; JPL-Caltech/STScI/CXC/SAO/O. Krause (Steward Observatory) 44-45; JPL-Caltech/University of Arizona 25cr; NASA/JPL 6-7cr, 27fcr (Neptune); SAO/CXC 45tc; K. Strassmeier (U. Wien)/Coude Feed Telescope/AURA/NOAO/NSF 43cl; Vacuum Tower Telescope/NSO/NOAO 20cl; WMAP Science Team 10tc, 11cb, 12cra; **Projeto Academia de Ciência:** Givanilson Góes 42bl; **Science Photo Library:** 24tr, 49cr; Richard Bizley 27bl; Chris Butler 12tl, 15fl, 33tr; Celestial Image Co./12br (Hydra); John Chumack 22-23tc; Detlev Van Ravenswaay 4cra, 13bc, 21bc, 55br, 55cr, 57cc; A. Dowsett, Health Protection Agency 11c; European Southern Observatory 10bc, 39cl; Mark Garlick 15tc, 40-41, 45ca, 45cb, 59clb; Tony & Daphne Hallas 32cra; David A. Hardy 11tc; Mehau Kulyk 48tc; Jon Lomberg 43bc; Andrew J. Martinez 23cl, 23cr; Steve Munsinger 29br; NASA 54cr, 57br, 57ra, 57tl; NASA/JPL 55tc; Ria Novosti 7tr, 54tl, 56cl; David Parker 10crb; Royal Astronomical Society 15bc, 33crb, 37cr; Royal Observatory, Edinburgh/AATB 12fbl (Virgo); John Santord 22-23c, 43bl; Friedrich Saurer 57crb; Science Source 15clb; Volker Steger 53c; US Geological Survey 14cl; Volker Steger/Max Planck Institute For Astrophysics 35bc; **SLAC National Accelerator Laboratory:** Marcelo Alvarez, John H. Wise and Tom Abel 8-9; **Sloan Digital Sky Survey (SDSS):** Michael Blanton and the SDSS Collaboration, http://www.sdss.org 35cr; **TopFoto. co.uk:** Ann Ronan Picture Library/HIP 12fbr; **José R. Torres:** 12bl (Corona Borealis); **Tao Yue:** Thomas Ruth, Modelmaker 54tc.